*"Brilliant Insights on health, happiness
and abundance in your life."*

D0661377

Prosperity Mind!

How To Harness The Power Of Thought

By Randy Gage

Gage, Randy.
    Prosperity mind! : how to harness the power of thought /
by Randy Gage. — 1st ed.
    p. cm.
    "Brilliant insights on health, happiness and abundance in
your life."
    LCCN 2003102889
    ISBN 0971557861

    1. Success—Psychological aspects.
    2. Self-actualization (Psychology) 3. Visualization.
    I. Title.

BF637.S8G34 2003   158.1
                          QBI33-1271

"Prosperity Mind" is part of a five-book series on Prosperity.

101 Keys to Your Prosperity

Accept Your Abundance! Why You are supposed to be Wealthy

37 Secrets About Prosperity

The 7 Spiritual Laws of Prosperity and How to Manifest them in Your Life

Prosperity Mind: How to Harness the Power of Thought

Published by:
Prime Concepts Publishing
A Division of Prime Concepts Group, Inc.
1807 S. Eisenhower Street
Wichita, Kansas 67209-2810 USA

Order Information:
To order more copies of this book, or to receive a complete catalog of other products by Randy Gage, contact:

Prime Concepts Group, Inc.
1-800-946-7804 or (316) 942-1111
or purchase online at:
www.RandyGage.com
www.Prosperity-Insights.com

What others are saying about Randy Gage . . .

"When I first met Randy I was broke, miserable, my health was on a downward spiral—and I didn't even realize it!

As a direct result of Randy Gage's prosperity coaching, I now—at the age of 30—have great relationships, drive a Viper, create wealth from my pool and take monthly vacations. I'm healthy, happy, and rich!

Here's the best part. Randy can do the same for you—if you allow prosperity into your life. He will show you how— step by step, smile by smile, dollar by dollar.

If you want the best of what life has to offer, devour everything Randy has to offer on Prosperity—do it TODAY!"

**– Art Jonak
CEO, NetworkingTycoon.com**

"Prosperity Mind! is the only book on how to create true happiness and abundance in your life you'll ever need. Read it until you understand, apply it until you have everything your heart desires! Yes, it's really that good!"

**– Michael S. Clouse
Author of *The Fifth Principle***

Dedication

To Reverend Bill Cameron, a true mystic and Biblical scholar, who taught me that you can't out give God.

Acknowledgements...

When I walked into the Unity on the Bay
Church in Miami, Florida, and heard Bill
Cameron for the first time, a whole new world
opened up for me. I began a voracious study
of the spiritual laws that govern prosperity that
continues to this day. This led me to a few
other reverends who brought great insight to
the process. Namely Charles Fillmore,
Ernest Holmes, Catherine Ponder and more
recently, Mike Murdock. I am in debt to all of
them for helping lead me to my assignment.

Table of Contents

Introduction

The note was scrawled across the back of a flyer for the chaplain program. It was written by a parishioner, right after a Sunday service I had given at my own church.

"I hadn't realized until you pointed it out that it's the rich people who are the spiritual ones," he wrote. *"I guess those slave holders were on the right track. The only thing wrong was the prosperity consciousness of those slaves!"*

No doubt the writer was being quite sarcastic, and thought his comments would expose the absurdity of my teaching, and support his beliefs. (Which, it's safe to assume, are that it is somehow spiritual to be poor, and that rich people are exploiting the poor.)

It's fascinating that he would pick such an analogy, because I DO believe that in many cases, rich people are operating at a higher consciousness than poor people. That's why they are rich!

I also believe people who allow others to steal their freedom have serious issues of prosperity consciousness. Since he didn't sign his note, he won't discover that instead of seeing irony in his comments—I see an element of truth. Imagine the amazement and shock he might feel. Perhaps you are feeling the same way now.

The fact that rich people have amassed wealth indicates that they are living by at least some of the spiritual laws that govern prosperity. <u>Of course, this does not mean that all rich people are spiritual and all poor people are not</u>. Prosperity is a synergy of a number of factors, including a strong spiritual connection, optimum health, great relationships, rewarding vocation, and, yes, the material aspects.

So, rich people who are sick, bitter and lonely are certainly not prosperous. By the same token, however, if you are healthy, spiritually grounded, have a great marriage, but struggle to pay your credit cards each month—you are certainly not prosperous either. And most certainly not experiencing the spiritual harmony your Creator is offering you.

In the book *"As a Man Thinketh,"* James Allen relates how usual it is for people to say, "Many men are slaves because one is an oppressor; let us hate the oppressor." He then goes on to note the increasing tendency of people to say, "One man is an oppressor because there are slaves; let us despise the slaves."

The real truth is that <u>both</u> the slaves and the oppressor are co-creators in ignorance, lack, and limitation. While it seems that they are victimizing each other—in reality, they are each victimizing themselves.

Prosperity and human dignity are both based upon value received. An oppressor cannot sustain prosperity because he is exacting more than he returns, and will ultimately bankrupt his own consciousness. A slave gives not enough value to himself, and likewise ends up in a state of spiritual bankruptcy. As the Course in Miracles teaches, there are no victims, only volunteers.

A person will remain weak, dependent and miserable by refusing to raise his or her consciousness. A person can reject servitude, conquer limitations, and achieve greatness by raising his or her consciousness. To quote again from Allen's book,

"A strong man cannot help a weaker unless that weaker is willing to be helped, and even then the weak man must be strong of himself; he must, by his own efforts, develop the strength which he admires in another. None but himself can alter his condition."

It's tough to develop the strength to be prosperous, if you're being continually programmed that it's spiritual to be poor. Especially if you're not even aware you're being programmed and it's on a subconscious level.

To experience true spiritual prosperity, you have to be manifesting prosperity in ALL areas of your life. Yet if you're doing ok in most areas, but you don't have much money—it's easy to fall into the trap our note writer did.

You want to believe that somehow your reward is coming later, heaven perhaps, and that you will in some way be compensated for living your current life of limitation. After all, who among us wants to believe that we are suffering needlessly, or have riches at our fingertips, but refuse to partake in them?

Of course you also have the data-sphere (TV, radio, newspapers, Internet, magazines, governments, religious institutions, etc.) programming you on a subconscious level that money is bad, rich people are evil, and it's spiritual to be poor. It's somehow comforting to think that Bill Gates, Ross Perot, Ted Turner, and all those other billionaires have sold their souls, and will one day get their just desserts.

Now to be fair to our letter writer—he certainly isn't alone. This kind of thinking is quite pervasive today.

So why would I write a book with a message, sure to threaten so many people? Because I fear what will happen to them when they are not threatened.

I take the privilege and the responsibility of my platform seriously. In fact, I consider it sacred. I speak the messages I perceive people *need* to hear, not necessarily the ones they *want* to hear. It pains me to see anyone anywhere experiencing poverty and lack in their life.

When you think about it, the idea of me giving a Sunday church service is kind of funny. I was raised atheist, and entered a church only twice in my first 30 years on the planet. (Once by accident, and once for a wedding.)

When I found my way to the church I would eventually call home, I was unemployed, had no car, was $55,000 in debt, and selling my furniture to eat. My health was shot; my relationships were an absolute mess; and I couldn't have been more unhappy. By the time the furniture was gone, and I was eating macaroni and cheese three times a day, I discovered a very fascinating thing . . .

I came to understand that success and prosperity had almost nothing to do with opportunities, chance, luck—or even training, education, or skill. It had everything to do with consciousness, beliefs, and even subconscious programming that you aren't aware of.

For the last few weeks, I've been having a dialogue via e-mail with my friend Stuart Goldsmith in London. Stuart attended one of my programs and used to publish an insightful newsletter in the U.K. on success.

He originally wrote me about his desire to create a work-at-home type of plan to help people get off government assistance and become independent. (He thought perhaps an envelope stuffing, assembly, or similar type of plan might work. One done honestly, not the many rip-off schemes that currently prey on these people.)

I want to share some of what I wrote him back on the subject of prosperity consciousness—because I think it's very relevant to what we are discussing here.

Some of what I write may strike you as uncaring, jaded, cynical, or heartless. However, once you understand the principles involved, you'll understand that my comments only come from wanting the highest good for others.

Try as I might to embrace Stuart's idea for a home work program for welfare recipients, it still reeks to me as rearranging deck chairs on the Titanic. Creating home work jobs for most of these people is like casting pearls before swine or whatever appropriate cliché you'd like to substitute. (See how cynical and uncaring I sound already!)

I still believe that it is true though, based on my own experience, and that of the "circle of losers," I associated with for the first 30 years of my life. You could have given any of us a home work program designed to make us a millionaire, and we would have snatched defeat from the jaws of victory.

Why?

Because we did not have the consciousness to be wealthy— or healthy—or happy. We were professional "victims."

When I started a business, the county started construction on the highway. The next time I had a crooked partner, and another time the economy went bad. Finally, the last time, the IRS seized my restaurant for non-payment of taxes, and auctioned it off on the courthouse steps. Which left me in the situation I mentioned earlier.

Which ultimately was the best thing that ever happened to me. By losing everything, I finally stopped looking at all the outside factors (crooked partner, IRS, economy, etc.), and started looking at the inside ones. Or, more specifically, asking the question, "Was there ONE person who was always at the scene of the crime?"

Of course I didn't like the answer I came up with, but it was the true one. All those outside factors were being manifested by me, because I:

- ❑ Had a subconscious fear of success;
- ❑ Lacked self-esteem; and,
- ❑ Didn't believe I was worthy of success.

It's very easy to cry victim and get your share of love, sympathy, etc. I was certainly the poster boy. And, of course, I surrounded myself with other victim friends who would commiserate with me. We would gather at every opportunity and share our tragedies with each other.

I would explain how those merciless, cold-blooded animals at the power company had shut off my lights, because I was one lousy day late. My friend Mike would top that with how he was getting evicted by his rich, heartless landlord. I would come back with how my license plate was impounded for unpaid parking tickets, and the battle would wage on.

And, of course, there is nothing worse than when your friends have a worse tragedy than you do! You have to immediately manifest a tumor, a meteorite landing on your car, or some other calamitous event to ensure that you get your proper share of sympathy.

Which is what I did for 30 years . . .

And before you disregard this as mystical fluff, I am talking about rational, scientific events here. Examples. You are attracted to another dysfunctional alcoholic spouse, choose another dishonest partner, open a business without doing the due diligence, spend your money on cigarettes and beer, but have none left to pay the rent, or a million other possibilities.

Yes it's true other people aren't getting thrown out on the street—but that's because they pay their mortgages. Yes, it's true that other people don't have their tire blow out on their way to the interview for that good job—but that's because they deferred getting cable TV and bought new tires when they needed them.

Poverty is not an absence of money and things—it is a mindset. Prosperity is not an abundance of money and things—it's also a mindset.

When I began studying the laws that govern prosperity, I embraced the principles out of desperation . . .

I applied those principles, and you'd be hard pressed to find anyone who has had a greater degree of turnaround. I am truly blessed, manifesting abundance in all areas of my life, in ever increasing ways.

This only happened because I was willing to confront my weaknesses, discover and eliminate the insidious "lack" programming I had, and replace it with positive programming. To this day, I am ever vigilant, mindful of what I allow myself to watch and listen to, and the people I associate with.

I had to get out of my comfort zone, brave fears, and face up to my beliefs. Once you have done this, you feel called to help others challenge the self-limiting beliefs that are holding them back from their greatness. That was the motivation I felt that morning, as I spoke at church, and the motivation that has me writing this book for you now.

Money is part of the magic in life. It is an enabling force that allows you to be the real you. It allows you to go where you wish to go, do what you wish to do, and become whom you desire to become. Money is God in action! Poverty causes people to lie, cheat, steal, and even kill. There is NOTHING spiritual about poverty. Yes, poverty really does suck.

Some of the people in my audiences are shocked when I make the statement that it is a sin to be poor. Of course, Charles Fillmore shocked the religious community of his day, when he made that proclamation almost 100 years ago. It still has the power to stun people today.

Yet if you learn the actual translation of sin, it means to "miss the mark." The Course in Miracles defines sin as a lack of love. I believe both characterizations are accurate.

If you are poor, you're missing the mark your Creator has set for you. And you're most certainly cheating yourself out of the love that is your birthright.

When you are providing true value to the universe— you are rewarded with riches.

That's the way the universe works. All the time, with no exception.

I recently read a newspaper op-ed piece by Ralph Nader— chastising Bill Gates and other billionaires for not redistributing their money to the poor people of the world.

Obviously, simple, underdog, fight-for-the-little-guy Nader (who is a multi-millionaire, by the way) doesn't understand even the most basic tenets of prosperity. If the top two percent of the richest people in the world were to redistribute their wealth to the bottom two percentile—within six months, the money would be right back where it started.

Why?

<u>Because of the consciousness of the people involved</u>. To become a billionaire, you have to first become the kind of person who can manage billions of dollars responsibly. You must be providing a great value to a great number of people, who are willing to trade some of their hard-earned money for that value.

Ayn Rand was one of the most brilliant thinkers in human history, a true genius, and someone who understood the concept of value for value. She wouldn't call it prosperity consciousness (she was a committed atheist), but she possessed it in spades. Her novel, "Atlas Shrugged," should be required reading, every year, for people concerned with prosperity. Another work of hers, and the one relevant here, is her book, "The Virtue of Selfishness."

When I speak to an audience, or write a book like this, I want people to understand a very simple, but very important thing. **They can't help anyone unless they have first helped themselves.** Or as Reverend Ike would say, the best thing you can do for poor people is not be one of them!

It doesn't serve God or you, if you are broke, sick, unhappy, or in dysfunctional relationships. You have to believe you are worthy of prosperity in ALL of its forms. Then as you walk the path of spiritual consciousness, you will find that you begin to manifest it more every day.

And that is what drives me to do what I do. So if I shock you, offend you, or threaten you with what I write—please evaluate why that might be. And know that I am coming from a place of love, and wanting the highest good for you. I want you to be healthy, happy and rich!

Randy Gage
Key West, Florida
March 2003

Chapter One
The Connection Between Thought & Circumstance

I was sitting along the creek, alone with my thoughts and the harmony that only the sound of running water can bring. The autumn chill was in the air, and the rustle of the breeze through the leaves added to the symphony of serenity.

A young woman was reading a book on my left, and an elderly gentleman was practicing Tai Chi about 30 feet away. A Suzuki motorcycle pulled up and parked at the edge of the street. The rider was dressed all in black leather, and had the look of a courier. He dismounted, removed a brown sack from his cargo box, and sat about 20 feet away from me. I spied him as he removed a cold chicken drumstick and some kind of sandwich, which he ate and chased with a bottle of Sprite.

It's October, in the south end of Dublin, Ireland, and I'm on the banks of the canal that runs under Baggot Street.

I chose to spend my lunch here, instead of at the five-star hotel where I am staying. Pigeons are strutting around me, and a young man is lying with his head nestled in the lap of his girlfriend. I didn't ask them, but I'll bet the other patrons in my creek-side café would agree that there isn't a restaurant in town that can rival the dining experience here.

Now the food at my hotel is great, but Ireland suffers from the same disease as the U.K. Namely that they think all restaurants should be gloomy caves, with dark mahogany wood and plenty of smoke. You'll find more windows in a submarine, than inside the average restaurant here.

So why am I at the canal, other than for obvious reasons?

I'm choosing the thoughts that create my circumstances—and the circumstances that will shape my life.

Take a trip to any jail or prison and you will meet hundreds of people who will tell you they are the victims of circumstances. Enter any big city ghetto or barrio and you'll see the same thing.

If you venture through some affluent, high-class WASP neighborhood in Connecticut, you'll discover the same thing. Likewise if you stroll through a middle-class neighborhood in London or Leeds, Cologne or Copenhagen. You will meet people who believe they are the result of their circumstances, good or bad.

They will talk about the opportunities they were given, or the chances they were denied. They may be grateful for the education they were exposed to, or bemoan the fact they were denied one. One person will celebrate his upbringing, while another will decry hers.

Yes, income, status, caste, education, upbringing, neighborhood, family and many other circumstances will influence, effect and even determine your station in life.

But who creates the circumstances?

Your parents? Your environment? God? Destiny? Lost in all this analysis and the assumptions of the people above is one very, very important reality:

The effect of thought on circumstance.

In "As A Man Thinketh," James Allen tells us that our minds are like a garden, which can be intelligently cultivated, or allowed to run wild. In either event, it will *bring forth*.

If you plant and tend your garden, it will produce flowers or fruits—the things you cultivate. If you don't plant specific seeds, then animals, wind and other elements will cause random things to fall into it, producing an abundance of weeds and wild vegetation, likely to choke out useful plants. One thing is certain. <u>Something will grow in your garden</u>.

Just as a gardener must tend his or her plot, keeping out the weeds, you must tend the garden of your mind, weeding out the thoughts of lack, limitation and negativity. You must nurture and tend the thoughts of happiness, success and purpose.

If you practice gardening of this kind, you will soon discover that you are the master gardener of your soul. You will come to the profound revelation that you are not the victim of your circumstances—but the architect of them. *For it is the thoughts that you give precedence to that shape your character, create your circumstances, and determine your ultimate destiny.*

Please read that last sentence again.

The outer circumstances and environment of your life are directly connected to your inner state. The most important thing you can learn about success, prosperity and happiness is that **thought and character are one.**

No one wakes up one day in prison, or divorce court, or the emergency room. It is the direct result of the thoughts you have had up to that point.

Now if you are like most people, this is the part where you start to mentally make excuses for yourself . . .

You believe that what I just said is true for *other* people most of the time, but you are quite certain that *you* have been the victim of extenuating circumstances beyond your control.

I know. Your situation is different. You're special . . .

OK you're allowed to think that. For a while. But let me tell you about me.

Because my situation was different. I was special . . .

I was in at least eleven negative, dysfunctional relationships because my partners were neurotic, excessively jealous and needy. They were always making demands on me because they couldn't meet their own needs.

In the first restaurant I owned, the guy I hired to run it was falsifying the sales figures and keeping 80% of the sales. This went on for almost four months before we caught him, long enough to put me out of business.

In the hair salon I bought, my partner actually stole the fixtures one weekend and sold them. The tax authorities seized the pizzeria I had.

In each case, I was just the innocent victim, manipulated and injured by others, always fighting against the circumstances, bad luck, etc.

Bullshit.

I chose those relationships; I hired that manager; I attracted my business partners, like I chose to start a business without enough capital and didn't pay my taxes.

You don't simply end up in jail or the hospital, bankrupt, or alone. No more than you simply wake up rich, successful, happy, and healthy. All these circumstances are the result of thousands of little decisions, which are reached as a result of hundreds of thousands of thoughts. The thoughts you give precedence to.

So just how does that work?

Well it pains me to even talk about it. It pains me because of the pain I see in people that I love. And it reminds me of the pain I used to have. And I hate to even think about that. But talk I must . . .

Some of you have heard the story I tell on my "Prosperity" audio album about the wake-up call I got one day in California. I had just had dinner with Spence and Shivani, a couple I respected a great deal. I had spent the meal doing what I always did at that time. I regaled them with all the bad breaks, poor luck, and unfortunate circumstances that had been happening to me. Afterward, as we were getting into their car, Spence said to me, "Have you given any thought to what you're doing to manifest all this?"

Well I was simply devastated. I couldn't believe how insensitive, uncaring, and clueless he was! I couldn't believe that he didn't understand and empathize with what an innocent victim I was.

I chewed on that for about three weeks before it finally dawned on me that Spence was right. And that's a very ugly realization to have.

But a very liberating one. Because once you get it—and you take ultimate responsibility for what is happening in your life—you start to think about how that really comes about.

I just got an email from someone two days ago. She has been struggling financially for quite some time. She has major health challenges, relationship issues, and some other drama going on. Now she writes to tell me that she was just in a serious car accident.

Another old friend of mine is struggling financially. He has been for the last five years I've known him, but this time, he just got laid off.

I'm quite sure that you know people in similar kinds of patterns. It wrenches your heart, but sometimes you have to step back and let them alone. The people I have talked about, I care about. But I can't help them yet. Because they don't understand this connection between thought and circumstance . . .

Sure I could send some money to the lady who was in the car accident. I will throw some business to my other friend anonymously. But I'm afraid these are just band-aids on a tumor. Because they will always need another check and another chance, until they make the connection we are talking about.

So let's talk about how all this applies to you.

First, you really do have to accept that on one level or another, you have manifested everything that is happening in your life. Even the horrific, nasty stuff.

Of course you don't do it consciously. But you do it.

I always believed that I wanted to be healthy. But I had allergy problems, a bad back, and a lot of other challenges that kept me sick. Most of them were hereditary. Or so I thought . . .

At that time, I had a hard time expressing love, and having it expressed to me. I didn't hug, say, "I love you," or other expressions of emotion. I wasn't psychologically able to, at that point in my life.

After the string of dysfunctional relationships, I finally got into therapy. It took me about three years, but I finally got to the point where I could express and accept love. An amazing thing happened . . .

My health problems all miraculously cleared up. I had been holding on to sickness, because on a subconscious level, that is how I believed you attracted loving attention. I didn't realize it then of course. But I know now, that that is exactly what was happening.

You can believe that you want to be successful, wealthy and powerful. Yet on a subconscious level, you may have some serious lack programming. So on this subconscious level, you may fear that if you get rich and successful, your family and friends won't like you anymore, or you won't fit in. So you could hold yourself back, and sabotage your own success.

Now here's the thing . . .

If you become successful, wealthy and powerful—IT IS QUITE POSSIBLE AND EVEN LIKELY that your family and friends won't like you anymore, and you won't fit in! At least that's what happened for me. But I was ok with that. Because I knew that my true friends wouldn't be bothered by my success, and would even celebrate it.

And I knew that if I wanted to "fit in," I needed to stay sick, broke and stupid.

Which I wasn't willing to do. So I changed a lot of things in my life, most importantly, the thoughts I give precedence to.

Which is why I am here at Baggot Creek, instead of the smoky restaurant at the Ballsridge Hotel. So where are you reading this? And how have you spent your day so far?

Chapter Two
Using the Power of Purpose

Ok I admit it. I have a charmed life. Everything I touch turns to gold. Or platinum. Or Prada.

I'm healthy, happy, and successful. My worst nightmare day is a lot of people's "dream come true."

Now it wasn't always this way . . .

For more than 30 years, my life sucked. Real bad. I was sick, unhappy, broke, and miserable. Everything I touched turned to camel dung. If anyone could snatch defeat from the jaws of victory, that would have been me.

So what changed?

The single most important thing—more important than anything else I have ever learned was this: <u>I came to the belief that I was responsible for everything that had happened in my life, both the good, and the unspeakable horrible</u>.

Which was a very frightening thought indeed . . .

Because it meant I could not blame my dysfunctional relationships on my partners anymore; I couldn't blame all my business failures on my sponsor, crooked partners, or the economy; and, I couldn't blame my poor health and other tragedies on God, the universe, destiny and circumstance.

And while that was quite a frightening thought at first . . . it became the thought that ultimately gave me freedom.

Because if all that was true about those bad things, then logic dictated that it must be true for the good things. Which meant that I could manifest being happy, getting rich, becoming successful, and attracting quality people into my life!

Do you really get this? Do you realize that you can manifest all the good things and live a life of health, happiness and prosperity?

Coming to this realization was the single, most important, defining breakthrough in my existence on this planet. Because it took me out of the mindset that I was a victim of circumstance, and created a mindset and belief that I could control my own destiny.

Now this thought is radically different from what most people believe. But then again, most people are sick, broke and stupid. They feel victimized by God, the Universe, nature, destiny, luck, circumstance, and a litany of other "outside" factors.

But when you feel these things victimize you, that discounts the very important reality of the effect your thought-forces and mind elements have upon our circumstances, character, and destiny.

You create your own circumstances by the thoughts you give precedence to.

So that is step one—working on the thoughts you give precedence to. But there is more.

Until your thought is linked with purpose, you can't experience the true prosperity that is your birthright.

I'm writing this chapter in the waiting room at the car dealership. Along with smelling the burnt coffee pot, everyone else is glued to the TV, watching a daytime talk show host. I don't think they have any idea of the insidious infection that is taking place.

Most people's thoughts are simply reactions to whatever is going on in the world around them. They have these random, aimless thoughts, and drift from one drama to another. They fall easy prey to gossip, petty worries and negativity. They are cogs in the matrix, lurching along with the herd. Daytime TV shows (and most nighttime ones) like the one that is on now, satiate this habit perfectly.

They have no purpose. Because they think taking care of themselves is selfish, and they think selfishness is bad, they attempt to make everyone else happy. Which of course leaves everyone most decidedly unhappy. So the closest thing they have to a purpose, is avoiding conflict, and making sure that no one else is too pissed off at them.

Not only must you have a purpose, but you also must make that purpose the central focus of your daily thoughts. You must make your purpose your supreme duty, with your eyes always on the target. When you do that, then you really do control the thoughts you give precedence to, and this creates your mindset. And it is your mindset that determines how successful you will really be in life.

Here's what the process looks like:

1) **Having an overriding purpose helps you direct your thoughts.**
2) **Those thoughts determine your mindset.**
3) **Your mindset determines how successful you will really be.**

How you will react to any situation that comes up is determined almost entirely by your mindset. Take my friend Matt. We stopped at a fried chicken joint to eat after our ball game one night. As we were walking to the door, he said, "You know what's going to happen? I bet they are going to be out of chicken! That happened to me once. I went in and they were out of chicken. How can a chicken place be out of chicken?"

So what happened?

We went in. I ordered a 3-piece chicken dinner, which I got. He ordered a 3-piece spicy chicken dinner. Which, of course they were out of. He looked at me and raised his arms, as if to say, "See? I told you so."

Now we could do a whole lesson on how he manifested their being out of chicken. But that's for another book. The point I'm raising here is his mindset.

He expects bad things to happen to him, so they usually do. I love him, but he affirms about 300 bad statements every day. I am constantly stopping him in mid-sentence, screaming, "Wait, don't affirm what you are about to say!" And he pauses for a second, thinks about it, and finally says something like, "Well it's true though. My suitcase is always the last one off the plane."

Fascinating, isn't it? Your mindset colors how you view every situation you encounter every day. And it shapes the way you attract things into your life.

Some people are predisposed to think they will be wildly successful; some figure they will get by; and others like Matt, expect the worst to happen. Your expectations will color how you view each situation you encounter, hundreds of times a day. That in turn will color how you act in each situation. And each one of those small, seemingly insignificant decisions determines your future.

If you think the rich get richer, and you have to have money to make money—you will probably do nothing to break out of being broke. You will think you want to be wealthy, but on a subconscious level, you will just be telling yourself it would be a wasted effort.

If you think that good things only happen to "other" people, you won't expect them to happen to you. And when they do, you won't even recognize them, because you're not expecting them. You won't accept people wanting to do good things for you. They may manifest as something simple, like refusing their offer to help you with a project, to something much larger, like refusing to accept love from someone who loves you.

You could pass up a great investment opportunity, decline to open a business that can make you wealthy, not protect your health, or even repel your perfect soul mate. Or all of the above.

Of course the opposite is true too . . .

If you believe you are worthy of wealth and happiness, you will expect good things to happen. And when they do, you will accept them gratefully. This is the power of autosuggestion, which operates in your subconscious mind.

When you are presented with lucrative opportunities, you are likely to act on them. And when you have a chance to try something really bold, daring and monumental—you will go for it!

So this leads to a fascinating area of speculation . . .

Namely whether you believe that we manifest cancer tumors, horrible accidents happening to us, people we love dying, and other horrible things. Or more specifically, do YOU believe that YOU manifest horrible things for YOU? Or do you think that they come from circumstance, fate and luck?

This may be the single most important question you ever ask yourself.

Because it means the difference between creating your destiny and spending a life of quiet desperation, reacting to drama, and challenges and a never-ending supply of misfortune.

Now does that mean that I think that you consciously or subconsciously wish upon yourself a tumor, or horrible accident or other tragedy?

No, not consciously anyway. But I do believe we can and do, attract bad things to us. <u>And I believe that we shape our circumstances by the power of thought</u>.

Now most people don't feel that way. It's a lot easier to believe in chance, luck, destiny, providence, and other outside factors. If we can blame things on God, nature, the universe, the economy and our asshole ex-spouse, it sure makes our misfortune more palatable, doesn't it?

But lost in all this is the very important reality of the effect our thought-forces and mind elements have upon our circumstances, character, and destiny.

So I don't think that you or I or anyone else would want to have a loved one die, or get into a horrible tragedy. But we can believe that we are not worthy and manifest a victim pattern. <u>Your soul attracts what it secretly harbors</u>.

That means that which it loves, and also that which it fears!

So that means you can reach the height of your greatest aspirations, goals and dreams, or sink to the level of your un-chastened desires. So that leads us to the million-dollar question for you.

Do you believe that your soul attracts what it secretly harbors? That which it loves, and also that which it fears? Or do you think I'm an uncaring, egotistical, arrogant, lucky, rich guy who forgot where he came from—and doesn't understand the special circumstances that aren't your fault that are holding you back?

How much responsibility did you accept for the last really bad thing that happened to you? (As in, getting fired or laid off from your job, being in a car accident, getting sick or injured, having a sinkhole appear under your master bedroom, etc.)

The amount of responsibility you take for this greatly determines your mindset, and thus how you might subconsciously attract and manifest bad things happening in your life.

If you are like most people, you admit that you are responsible for a lot that takes place in your life. You agree that you are your thoughts, and that your thoughts create both your character and your circumstances.

But . . .

You probably would add something like, "Surely Randy you don't think that I had anything to do with (fill in the blank)." Well I'm not going to be the one to tell you that you manifested getting an incurable disease, losing a loved one, going bankrupt, or any of a hundred other unspeakable calamities that may have happened to you. And you probably wouldn't believe me if I did.

But I know this . . .

I didn't want to be in jail at 15, but I was there as a result of the actions I took. I didn't want to be sick, broke and stupid, but I was, because of the thoughts I gave precedence to. I didn't want to have my business seized by the tax authorities, but that was a direct result of my actions. And I certainly did not want to get shot, but even that was a direct result of some decisions I made, and the mindset I had at the time.

I do know that when I changed my mindset, I changed my own life.

So here's the other side of the question . . .

How much responsibility did you accept for that last wonderful, glorious thing that happened in your life? (As in finding the love of your life, your child being born, getting the promotion, making a big profit on an investment, etc.)

Here's why I ask . . .

If you think all the good things come from good luck, destiny or—dare I say this, God—you could be missing out on a lot of good things. Now before the fundamentalists burn this book, let me explain . . .

In the form of a story.

A farmer was in the fields, tending his crops when a passerby struck up a conversation. He mentioned to the farmer how blessed he was that God had given him such a beautiful farm.

The farmer mentioned how he had repainted the barn and the farmhouse, and the stranger again remarked how God had blessed him.

The farmer talked about how he had removed all the rocks and tree stumps to plow the fields. The stranger smiled and nodded, and remarked again how God had blessed the farmer. This went on for some time, with the farmer talking with pride about the improvements he had made, and the stranger repeating how God had blessed the farmer. Finally, in exasperation, the farmer exclaimed, "You should have seen the place when I took it over from God!"

There is an important prosperity lesson in this parable. If you believe in God, I'm happy for you. But don't give away all your power and responsibility! God—or the universe, or whatever forces you believe in—can only do FOR you, what he can do THROUGH you.

You were given free choice. You were given the abilities to manifest the things you dream about. But as the Quakers like to say, "As you pray, move your feet."

God gave me the ability to play softball, which brings much pleasure to me. But if I wanted to do it at a high level, I knew that I would have to practice, do drills, learn the intricacies of the game, and get in better aerobic shape. So I did.

God gave Pavarotti a beautiful gift. But do you have any idea how hard he worked (Pavarotti, not God) to refine and develop that gift?

While it is important to take responsibility for the bad things in your life, it is just as important, to take responsibility for the good things!

Because if you don't take some credit for the good things—you don't have the mindset that you can actually create more of them. Think about it. And think about the credit you deserve for what you do.

As I told you—I don't think that you or I or anyone else would want to have a loved one die, or get into a horrible tragedy. I didn't want negative relationships, to get evicted from my apartment, to get shot in a robbery, to have addictions, to end up in jail, or to get sick. But I do believe that I manifested ALL of those things by the mindset I had at the time.

I was in the ultimate victim pattern for 30 years. And I was continually manifesting proof on a daily basis that I was an unlucky, unfortunate guy who just couldn't catch a break. Of course that was all bullshit.

I was riddled with guilt, low self-esteem and feelings of unworthiness, and I kept manifesting drama to satiate my need for feeling worthy in lieu of being the simple, poor, but spiritual guy, who was fighting the forces of evil and oppression. I am so glad I don't have to do that anymore!

So what about YOU? What kind of mindset do you have toward prosperity?

You are a being of free thought, critical thinking and love. You are the lord of your thoughts, and therefore hold the key to your mindset. The transforming and regenerative mindset that allows you to make of yourself what you will. So that means you can reach the height of your greatest aspirations, goals and dreams, or sink to the level of your un-chastened desires. So think about the most important question you'll ever answer, and we'll look at how you can create a better mindset, next.

Chapter Three
Changing Your Mindset

Prosperity Mind is not an accident. It is cultivated daily. I was on the phone with a friend from Texas last night. He asked about a mutual friend we have. "He's been exposed to you a lot," he said. "Why do you think he keeps sabotaging himself?"

"You know what?" I replied. "He really hasn't been that exposed to me. He's been to three or four of my seminars. But he's not on Breakthrough U (my coaching program). So he spends five or six hours with me once a year, and then he goes back to thousands of hours worth of counter-programming. He never had a chance."

And that's a shame.

The guy we're talking about has been working hard to succeed in a variety of different businesses for the last ten years. And I mean he works hard. And means well. And he wouldn't intentionally hurt a flea.

Yet I've seen him crash and burn four times in that time span. The latest meltdown was a few weeks ago.

And he is a bright guy. Universally well-liked, and he never stole a freight train. So why does he keep failing?

Two things come to mind, and they're both relevant to what we are talking about here. They both are a big part of your mindset, and the kinds of changes you have to make in it to move from *victim* to *victor.*

The first problem with my friend is that he refuses to live by one of the universal laws of prosperity. That is the concept of trading value for value. Or put another way, the only free cheese is in the mousetrap. Like a lot of people today, he has an entitlement mindset. He sees that he is struggling and others are not. So he thinks it's only fair that they should somehow provide for his advancement.

So he is continually aligning in business relationships with people who have more resources than he does. Each of these arrangements is supposed to enrich both parties, but they always end up coming up short. There is always just enough to pay his expenses, but nothing left for the other partners.

Now he doesn't do this maliciously, or deceptively—or even consciously. He just always comes up a little short and he regales you with his tales of woe. And you look into his big brown eyes and you offer to give up your profit if it will help him out.

Or at least that's what I did . . .

The first time. So I naturally thought that being his patron saint the first time around, he would work to ensure that I was taken care of in round two.

That was a $25,000 lesson for me. One that I don't need to learn any more, thank you very much. But this isn't about me. The subject was why this individual keeps snatching defeat from the jaws of victory. And that takes us to the second issue . . .

Self-sabotage.

Now this guy certainly doesn't see it that way. He sees it as a whole chain of unlucky outside circumstances. He blames the economy, his partners and other external factors. He is certain that he wants to be successful, so the possibility that he could actually be sabotaging his own success doesn't even occur to him. And if you were to suggest it, he would brush it off without so much as a cursory thought.

Like most people—he evaluates everything about himself based on the evidence of his conscious mind.

And what a foolish mistake that is. Millions of people self-sabotage themselves daily. <u>And most of them are not even aware of it</u>.

Their rational, logical conscious minds tell them that they want to be healthy, happy and prosperous. Let's face it. Who wouldn't?

But then why are so many people sick, depressed and broke?

Because on a subconscious level—they don't believe they are worthy. Perhaps their church, temple or synagogue programmed them that they were a worm by the time they were eight years old. Maybe their parents got divorced when they were ten and they thought it was their fault. Perhaps their father worked ten hours a day in a tough manual labor job, and now they feel guilty for earning more money than he did.

They spent hours a day, plopped in front of the television. So you can safely assume that they were completely brainwashed by the media by the time they were ten years old. They have learned:
- ❑ Rich people are pompous, conniving and dishonest;
- ❑ Poor people are the salt of the earth; and,
- ❑ It is somehow noble, decent, and spiritual to be poor.

We could come up with a thousand reasons they may be programmed for lack and limitation. And a thousand reasons that you may be. Now like my friend I described earlier, you may have attended a couple seminars of mine, read some positive books and set goals for positive outcomes. *But do you know how many thousands of hours of counter-programming you are still receiving?*

Are you really screening the books you read? Did you eliminate the news outlets? Have you stopped watching 90% of the shows on television? Did you eliminate all radio talk shows from your diet? Do you excuse yourself from the conversation when it turns to gossip, lack and negativity? Have you replaced former friends and acquaintances in your life that were negative? Do you schedule and restrict the time you spend with negative family members?

If you didn't answer "yes" to ALL of these questions, I worry about the tremendous amount of lack programming you are being exposed to on a daily basis. If you did answer "yes" to all of the above, what that means is that you are likely getting "only" about fifty exposures to negative programming a day!

So in either case—what are you doing to counteract this programming?

It may be much more important than you know. It is that constant daily programming you receive that determines your mindset. And it is your mindset that determines your eventual level of achievement in everything you do.

Example. Suppose you get offered a chance to participate in a business opportunity. You could approach this in a number of different ways, each one would be dependent on your mindset.

You could jump in blindly, without doing any research, just because you are enamored with the idea of getting rich. You could enter a very bad situation and lose a lot of money. This happens to people every day.

Or scenario two, you could figure that any deal you find out about is already too late. You could figure the "insiders" get all the sweetheart deals and it's probably much too good to be true. So you pass up the chance to buy Microsoft when it's $10 a share.

Another scenario occurs when you get offered a situation; you have confidence in yourself; you study it thoroughly; and you make a sound decision.

There are other possible scenarios, but you get the idea. How you will react to it is determined almost entirely by your mindset. You are made or unmade by your mindset.

It's important to remember that your mindset and expectations will be determined by the thoughts you give precedence to. James Allen equated your mind to a garden.

If you leave the garden uncultivated, whatever the wind blows in—plants, weeds or whatever—is what grows there. If you consciously plant it, and cultivate it—you keep it weeded and grow the flowers, fruits, or vegetables you desire.

If you don't screen out the kind of stuff we discussed earlier, those will be the weeds that blow in and choke out your prosperous, healthy and happiness thoughts.

People often ask me when their self-development work and personal growth will finally "take," and they will stop having negative thoughts. I wish I knew. Although I'm afraid the answer could be never.

Remember all the screening suggestions I mentioned a while back. I do every single one of them. In addition, I play CDs with positive subliminal messages while I sleep each night. I start each day by reading something positive, and end each night the same way. I have many positive, success-oriented people in my life. I feast regularly on positive books, tapes and other programs. And let me tell you what happened yesterday . . .

I have an embarrassing confession to make.

I was practicing the vacuum law of prosperity in my closet again. I decided that since I have so many nice, stylish and beautiful clothes—I was going to stop wearing blue jeans so often. The last time I did this, I gave away over 40 pair of jeans. I still had about 15 left.

About five of them are black Armani, Boss, or other designer jeans that I could wear with a sport coat or a similar "casually elegant" situation. That still left me with ten pair of blue jeans. I made a spur-of-the-moment decision to give away nine of them. I figured that way I couldn't be lazy and just reach in the closet and grab a pair every day. So I stacked the nine pair up on my donation pile. And then it came . . .

The thought.

For a fleeting moment I thought about what would happen if I lost everything and had to start over again. I remembered the time when the tax authorities seized my business, and I took a job in a diner, as a breakfast cook to get by. So I had this momentary thought about the possibility that I might ever have to take a manual labor job where I would want to have those blue jeans again.

And that blows my mind.

For the sake of this neurotic fantasy, let's suppose I lost everything tomorrow. Everything.

I could start a restaurant chain (which I already have the concept for) and would likely become a billionaire. I need just to snap my fingers and I could have ten or twenty investors. I could restart my speaking and seminar business and make millions of dollars from scratch.

I could announce that I was available for copywriting projects and pull in a million dollars a year. I could jump back into network marketing and be worth a couple million in a few years.

I could announce my availability as a marketing consultant and have more business than I could possibly handle. If I mentioned to my Mastermind Council that I was looking for a job, I would have two or three high five-figure offers to run companies in five minutes.

Truth is, it wouldn't matter what business I do, I would be successful in it.

But I still had that thought . . .

Fleeting, though it was. And I have been working on my prosperity consciousness for 13 years! I've made millions of dollars, and I have the ability to make billions more. I judiciously guard against negative programming to the point that I will leave a movie halfway through, or end a conversation in mid sentence if I don't like the direction it is going. *And I still had that thought.*

And you know what?

I've had lots of other ones. Sometimes ten a day. As rich, successful, healthy and happy as I've become, I have often still had fear-based thoughts. Looking back now, I see a lot of things I did, thinking they were prosperous, but I see now that they were fear-based.

When I bought a bike, I bought a titanium professional race bike for $3,000. I remember thinking then that if things got bad, I could always sell it for some quick cash.

Well I bought four sports cars at the same time, and I felt secure, knowing I could always sell one or two and scrape together a hundred grand.

Coming from the place I did, I always felt like I was somehow cheating destiny. That God, or the universe, or someone was going to wake up one day and discover that I had acquired wealth by mistake.

And given my mother's proclivity for worst case, nuclear meltdown scenarios, I still had that niggling thought in the back of my mind—the defensive, better-prepare-for-the-really-bad scenario, and have my options covered—just in case. And not get my hopes up too high—because then I would be setting myself up for a great disappointment. And like I told you, I've had those kinds of thoughts recently, as many as ten a day.

But here's the difference . . .

I notice every one of them now. Immediately. And I often laugh about how silly they are. Best of all, I see the progression of my mindset.

First, I had hundreds of negative thoughts a day, and noticed none of them.

Then I graduated to the point that I had lots of negative thoughts a day and noticed some of them.

From there I got to the point where I had fewer negative thoughts a day and I noticed lots of them.

And gradually over time, I started having fewer and fewer of them. Some days I have none. And now when I do have them, I catch myself right away.

I used to wear a rubber band on my wrist, and snap it when I had a lack thought. Now I no longer need to do that. I just tap my fingers on my forehead. That's the signal to my mind, and I instantly reject that thought, and replace it with another one. And once that happens, the world changes.

So when do the negative thoughts end? I don't know that they ever do. The sheer enormity of how much negative and lack programming you will be assaulted with over the course of a lifetime makes that seem unlikely. (But let's not affirm that!)

When you really analyze and think about this regularly— you will start to notice these thoughts. And once you do that, they lose most of their power.

And your mindset starts to change . . .

You change your core fundamental beliefs. You believe you are supposed to be healthy, happy and prosperous. You believe you are worthy. And when you are confronted with dozens of situations each day, most minor, some bigger, and even some that are major—you expect good things to happen to you!

You expect to find that tie you need to complete the perfect outfit; you anticipate winning in a sporting event; you figure you are next in line for that promotion; and you expect your business ventures to be successful.

In any event, if you keep counter-programming—you will win the fight. Because once you control the programming—you control the mindset. And once you control the mindset—you control your destiny!

Chapter Four
Sexual Alchemy

Sex contains all, bodies, souls,
Meanings, proofs, purities, results.
promulgations,
Songs, commands, health, pride, the maternal
Mystery, the seminal milk,
All hopes, benefactions, bestowals, all the
Passions, loves, beauties, delights of
The earth.

-Walt Whitman

In "Think and Grow Rich," Napoleon Hill lists the ten ways
to stimulate your mind. They are:

1) The desire for sex expression.
2) Love.
3) A burning desire for fame, power, or financial gain.
4) Music.
5) Friendship.
6) A Master Mind alliance.
7) Mutual suffering, such as that experienced by
   people who are persecuted.
8) Autosuggestion.
9) Fear.
10) Narcotics and alcohol.

Well I can conclusively say that Napoleon was right,
because I have researched them all! And each of the
things on that list really does have the power to stimulate
your mind in new and exciting ways. Unfortunately, not
everything on the list is for your highest good.

Alcohol and other drugs have done much to stimulate creative people. Edgar Allen Poe wrote "The Raven" under the influence; Hemmingway never met a bar stool he didn't like; and lots of other writers did their best work intoxicated. Janis Joplln, Jimi Hendrix and Jim Morrison made amazing music under the influence of drugs. But ultimately, this stuff destroyed them all.

I used to love the creative high I got from smoking marijuana. But what's the point of stimulating your brain, if you have to kill brain cells to do it? I used to feel uninhibited and social when I did certain hard drugs or got drunk. But the hangovers and the letdowns weren't worth the price.

I tried the burning desire for fame and power too. But once you go through therapy and get rid of your baggage, it really isn't that much fun to run the world anymore. Ultimately, this stimulation, like the previous one, ends up being destructive.

Fear is the other stimulus that is on the edge. I think a little fear can be helpful. If we're afraid we will miss a promotion, it may motivate us to do a better job on a project. If we fear losing someone special in our life, we may treat him or her with more respect, love and appreciation. But when the fear gets too great, it moves from natural and constructive, to negative and destructive.

I've certainly done the mutual suffering and persecution thing too. There really is some strength in that, believe it or not. After Hurricane Andrew struck Florida, I was amazed at the way people stepped in and helped each other. You saw a similar reaction after the September 11th terrorist attacks. But who wants to go through suffering for more stimulation?

The other issue in this, is that the stimulation can quickly turn negative . . .

I used to hang around all day commiserating with my victim friends. We would spend all our time together ruminating on our bad luck, the unfairness of the world, and other injustices. We formed a strong bond. In actuality, what we had was a Mastermind for misery. And it worked!

So now we have four ways to stimulate our minds, but each with some serious drawbacks. That leaves us six on the list. Each is positive and each can help you. But one of them, the desire for sexual expression, is greater than all other nine items on the list combined.

Sexual energy is the most powerful driver we have. It has the potential to power you to great achievement, or drive you to utter failure. Here is what we know about it.

Sexual energy in animals is all encompassing. Watch the mating rituals of spiders; see the force of fornicating lions; or witness when a stallion is brought in to sire a mare, and you will see driving and consuming purpose like nothing else. It is one of the most powerful energy forces in nature, on par with an earthquake or a hurricane.

In man, sexual drive is moderated by conscious thought. Most of the time anyway. When you are driven by sexual desire you can harness creativity, energy and imagination unknown to you at any other time. This drive is so strong many a person has risked their reputation and even their life to indulge it.

This sexual energy you have is quite natural, and you should nurture it. This drive cannot be submerged, and it is foolish to try. Nor should you want to. It is a healthy innate part of who you are. There are two ways to satiate this powerful desire . . .

The first way is of course, physical release. This is a healthy part of human existence, and is quite natural. But like anything good for you, too much of it sends it to the other side of the equation. A sex-crazed person is no different than a drug-crazed one. They both are addictions that can ruin your health and your life.

When you reach orgasm, you release a tremendous amount of sexual energy from your body. This energy is actually "Chi," the force of life. It takes a certain amount of time to replenish this energy, and this time span increases as you age. One of the best investments you will ever make in your health, longevity and prosperity will be learning some tantric sex techniques.

You will bring variety, meaning and more intimacy to your lovemaking, and both you and your partner will help to replenish energy with each other quicker. You will also learn how to have enjoyable sexual relations without orgasm, and men can learn how to have orgasm without ejaculation. Learning these techniques will stimulate and enhance your sexual energy, and greatly reduce the life force you deplete.

This is all assuming that you are enjoying sexual relations with someone you love. Remember that there is a difference between sex and love. Sex is biological, while love is spiritual. When you combine the two, you have an experience that touches your heart while it stimulates your loins, and creates an exponentially more powerful experience.

Recreational sex is simply biological, and cannot provide the same nourishment for your mind, body and soul, and thus can't further your prosperity journey.

I won't lie to you. I have had my share and a lot more, of exotic, erotic recreational sex. I grew up in the free sex 70s, and I have explored many avenues in the sexual universe.

I can tell you that when I was engaging in frequent promiscuous sex, my energies were dissipated, and I did not have the focus I needed for success in other areas of my life.

I am not going to get into the morality of recreational sex. That is not the purpose of this book, nor is it the basis of this discussion. That is a personal issue for you, best left to you. I broach the subject here, only in the context of making you aware that this kind of sex is very depleting to your life energy.

My great success in life came when I learned how to transmute my sexual energy into other productive areas. And that is the second way to release the tremendous sexual energy you have . . .

Becoming a sexual alchemist.

Alchemy, if you remember, is the ancient science of transforming base metals into gold. Sexual alchemy is the science of transforming base desires into driving energy to accomplish other things. When you harness your sexual energy and transmute it along these lines, you channel imagination, courage, creativity, drive and determination in previously untapped levels. It is a powerful force for prosperity, when properly channeled.

If you channel some of this energy to outlets, you can make massive strides toward your prosperity. If you don't, this energy will be released only through physical channels, and deplete your life force. Here's what else Napoleon Hill says on the subject in "Think and Grow Rich."

"Sex energy is the creative energy of all geniuses. There never has been, and never will be a great leader, builder or artist lacking in this driving force of sex."

Now this is not to say that everyone who is highly sexed is a genius. You attain this state of genius only when you stimulate your mind so it draws upon all the resources available to it for growth and creativity. You can't simply have sexual energy. It must be transmuted from desire for physical release to another form of desire and action. That is when your efforts are lifted to genius levels.

After extensive research, Hill discovered that the vast majority of successful men reached their success after age 40, and often after age 50. The conclusion of the study was that the vast majority of men dissipated their energies through overindulgence in sexual activity.

Most people never discover that their sexual urges have other possibilities, and that's why there are so many sick, broke and unhappy people. Once people understand this reality, noteworthy achievements immediately follow.

In the book, Hill lists people of outstanding achievement whose history and biography testify that they were of a highly sexed nature. This list includes such notables as George Washington, Thomas Jefferson, Napoleon Bonaparte, Elbert Hubbard, William Shakespeare, Ralph Waldo Emerson, Enrico Caruso, and others. These men, and many other people like them, were able to transmute their sexual energy into other productive avenues.

Obviously, I would recommend a reading or re-reading of "Think and Grow Rich" for any serious prosperity student. I would also recommend a book by my friend Felice Dundas entitled, "Passion Play." Felice is a doctor of Chinese medicine, and her book is a marvelous look at how to deepen intimacy, and harness your sexual energy for pleasure, vitality and healing.

Now transmuting your sexual energy into other pursuits takes a tremendous amount of willpower. Most people are unwilling to make this sacrifice. But extraordinary prosperity comes from extraordinary achievement, creating extraordinary value for others. And such achievements require sacrifice.

Powerful intellectual and creative achievements are attained from consecrated thought, focused on the search for knowledge. If you will sacrifice some of your confused animal thoughts and concentrate them on the development of your plans, the rewards will be astonishing.

Chapter Five
Programming Your Subconscious Mind

Every thought that reaches your conscious mind, gets transferred to your subconscious mind for filing. This becomes your "hard drive," and your conscious mind draws on it for all the decisions you make. This is done automatically, and often without effort or deliberation.

So for example, maybe when you were quite young, one of your parents said something like, "Those rich people are always trying to chisel out of their taxes." At that age you are very impressionable, and very protective of your parents. You're not even sure what rich people are, but you know that they are trying to do something to hurt your parents.

So later if they say something like, "We may be poor, but at least we're honest," it's another piece of programming on your hard drive. You don't even know it's there. Because as you get older, you come to the conclusion that you want to be rich. So you may work two jobs, save money for a business, and do all kinds of things to get wealthy.

Unbeknownst to you, you have programming on your hard drive that will stop you. It's a small voice that you can't even hear, and it's saying things like, "You'd better stop what you are doing, or you are going to be rich. And if you're rich, your parents won't love you anymore; you won't fit in with your friends; and you'll have to sell your soul. You'd better stop doing what you're doing right now."

You never hear this voice, but it can subconsciously sabotage what you are trying to do nonetheless.

You're getting this kind of negative programming, 24 hours a day, seven days a week from the data-sphere (TV, radio, movies, Internet, friends and family). And if you aren't censoring some of these sources, and replacing them with positive counter-programming, the sabotage cycle continues.

But it can be stopped . . .

You can program your own subconscious mind. This is what we mean by autosuggestion. It simply means all self-administered suggestions and stimuli, which reach your mind through your five (arguably six) senses.

The thoughts you give precedence to in your conscious mind, determine what gets filed for saving in your subconscious mind. So the first place you start is with the conscious stuff you are aware of. If you are a prosperity-conscious person, you won't watch 95% of the programs on network television. You wouldn't watch talk shows and reality shows that take advantage of people's ignorance for your entertainment. You wouldn't read 95% of the books on the bestseller lists. Most of the Hollywood movies that come out wouldn't be on your must-see list, and you'd be very selective about whom you spend time with. You would be always vigilant about everything that has the power to program your subconscious mind.

But that isn't enough . . .

Not by a long shot. You have to be very proactive about giving yourself positive programming as well. I keep a little publication called "Daily Word," and the book "As a Man Thinketh," next to my bed, everywhere in the world I am. That way, the first thing in the morning, and the very last thing before I turn off the light, I read a short passage of something positive. I want that positive message imprinting itself on my subconscious mind.

I believe in affirmations. I say them out loud; I write them out 13 times; and I sometimes put them on stickers around the house, so I see them all the time. I believe in having goal cards, or writing goals and positive statements in your planner. Every time you see them, even if it is just out of the corner of your eye, they are making an impression on your subconscious mind.

One of my favorite activities, and something that worked great for me, is building a Dream Board. This is a big piece of poster board that you fill with pictures, affirmations and other things you want to manifest in your life. (For instructions on how to do this, read book four in this series "The 7 Spiritual Laws of Prosperity and How to Manifest Them in Your Life.") Then you put this someplace where other people won't see it (so negative people can't ridicule it), but you see it every day. Like the other things, just walking by and seeing it out of your peripheral vision has an effect on you.

In book two in the series ("Accept Your Abundance"), I share a powerful programming technique from seminar leader Richard Brooke. He has you actually write a movie script of the thing you want to manifest.

Here's what you must understand about your subconscious mind. It doesn't question, argue, or doubt. It does exactly what it is programmed to do, no questions asked. It responds very well to imaginary scenarios. So when you affirm things like, "I am in perfect health," it works to make that true.

Here's the secret . . .

The more real you make things, and the stronger you imprint them, the faster your subconscious mind can make them come true in reality. So what you want to do is involve as many of your senses as you can. That's why Richard's movie script idea works so well. You can write all senses into the script. So you can wake up, smell the coffee downstairs, hear the waves crashing on the shore, feel the pride as you receive the Academy Award, touch the hair of your soul mate, and see the sunrise over the water, from the view in your penthouse. *The more real you make it—the sooner it becomes real!*

I have one more technique to share with you. And it is a powerful one! It's a way to directly program your subconscious mind with the exact information you want it to have.

Another interesting aspect to know about your subconscious mind is that it goes through cycles, and during certain of these cycles, it is more susceptible to being programmed.

The perfect time to program your mind is when you are in an "Alpha" state. Alpha is the state of deep relaxation—the state you feel right before you drop off to sleep, or when you are gently waking up in the morning. By the time you're halfway through the massage you're getting, you're probably in a wonderful Alpha state. But it can be difficult to be programmed at those times.

So here's the perfect time . . .

Meditation. When you get in a deep meditative state, you are in alpha cycle. Now if you haven't been trained in meditation, let me give you a way to get into a deep meditative state, almost at will.

First, get into a relaxed position, usually sitting down, with your legs crossed, or on a chair. Close your eyes, and begin breathing deeply. Breathe in through your nose, and exhale out your mouth. Slow, steady deep breaths.

Begin counting backwards from 50, with each exhalation. Clear your mind of outside thoughts, and just concentrate on the next number. If stray thoughts come into your mind, just notice they are there, then release them and go to your next number.

Starting at 50, you will be in a deep Alpha state by the time you get to one. You now can start programming your subconscious mind. Best to do this in the form of affirmations. Examples:

Money is attracted to me like a magnet.

I make wise food choices and find time to exercise.

My perfect soul mate is attracted to me now.

I am a Diamond Director with XYZ Company.

I am a multi-millionaire.

Now to the uninitiated, making affirmations like these is corny, or even silly. They have no idea how wrong they are. This is a POWERFUL programming technique.

Once you have completed all the things you want to program, then say something like the following:

"I am going to count backwards from five to one. When I reach one, I will return to an awake, alert state, refreshed and ready for a great day. Five...I am starting to hear what

is going on around me. Four...my eyelids are feeling lighter. Three...I am feeling alert. Two...."

That's what you might do if you were meditating in the morning. If you were doing it at night, you might say something like this:

"I am going to count backwards from five to one. When I reach one, I will be relaxed and serene, ready for a good night's sleep. Five...I am starting to feel sleepy. Four...my eyelids are feeling heavy. Three...."

Now if you are nervous or you're afraid you wouldn't be able to remember what to say when you're in the Alpha state, make a tape! You can just sit relaxed, with your finger on the tape player. Start counting backwards, and when you get to one, push the 'Play' button. You'll have exactly the affirmations you want, in your own voice.

Remember this. Your subconscious mind doesn't analyze or critique. It simply runs on autopilot, doing what it is programmed to do. These autosuggestion techniques allow you to choose the programming you want—which leads to the exact results you want to manifest!

Chapter Six
The Siren Song of Satisfaction

It was a Saturday evening, and we were having a dinner party at the home of one of my Mastermind Council members. The topic of conversation turned to complacency. Or more specifically mediocrity.

Falling into a comfort zone. Settling for good, when we know we can be great.

One of the guests was a good friend who wants to be a speaker. Or so he says. He even attended my last Speakers Institute, where it became obvious that he is an engaging presenter, has a lot of information to share, and should probably be doing exactly that.

At the Institute he outlined a number of things he wanted to do, products he wanted to develop, and workshops he could conduct. I even encouraged him to join the Mastermind Council, because I thought the intellectual and creative stimulation is exactly what he needs to bust loose.

He never joined, saying he needed the money for a house he was buying. In fact, he has never even joined at the beginner level. Like a lot of my friends, he figures he talks to me all the time, so why pay money to join something like that? (Just another manifestation of the hometown prophet syndrome.)

In the year and a half since the Institute, he has done exactly nothing to further his dream. What happened?

Life. Or more specifically, the day-to-day "busy-ness" of life. He's in his new house, active with his profession, and doing all the things we all do.

But we all do those things. Yet some of us still find the time to pursue our dreams.

What's the difference?

Now another friend was supposed to join us that night, but he had to cancel. He is already a professional speaker. For the last two years he has been chatting with me about repositioning his business to face the changing realities of the marketplace. We explored it a while back, and I gave him an informal "Hot Seat," creating some recommendations for what he could do. I think what I came up with has a lot of potential in the market, and could prove to be quite lucrative for him.

He has yet to move forward on it, opting instead to wait back and see if something else will develop. He talks about it a lot, and keeps reanalyzing the situation, but hasn't taken any action to move forward.

So what's holding him back?

I think the answer is similar for him as it is for my other friend. <u>Like it is for you and me</u>. Sometimes we are hungry, but we're not HUNGRY. Sometimes the siren song of the status quo seduces us. This is lack programming at work.

At the dinner party the other night, my friend kept saying things like, "If you saw how far I've come already," and "Compared to where I was a few years ago . . . "

And that's where the danger is . . .

Validation. Golden handcuffs. Because we are not starving in the street, we sometimes can get complacent with our circumstances. You may want more out of life, but if you are moderately comfortable with your current state, you might not be motivated enough to really dig in and attempt something bold, daring and challenging.

Now a lot of people will simply say, "So What? What's wrong with that? If you've reached a certain level of success, why not take some time to smell the roses; to be grateful for what you have; to be satisfied with what the Lord has given you . . . blah, blah, blah?"

Because that is a crime against nature. Your nature. Your nature as a human to grow, develop, and unfold into your greatest good.

There is nothing sadder and more tragic—than untapped human potential. For untapped potential—no matter what level you are at—is an acceptance of mediocrity. And a denial of your greatness.

This holds true at any level.

If Alex Rodriquez is happy being the 10th greatest baseball player in the league—that's mediocrity. Because he has the skills to be the best.

Now you could say that even at number ten, Alex is still better at baseball than six billion people, and he is in the 99.99 percentile. But for him to settle for the 10th best would still be mediocrity for him, because he is the best baseball player alive today.

Tiger Woods could decide to train less, take things easier, and settle for being the second or third best golfer on the circuit. And you know what? For him, that would be settling for mediocrity.

It's easy to give in to the siren song of satisfaction. And we all do it from time to time, in different areas of our lives. And that's ok, we have to. We can't be our absolute best in every single thing we do in this world, or we will drive ourselves crazy.

But there are some areas that are hills to die on.

And knowing which hills these are, is the secret to living a life of meaning, prosperity, and fulfillment.

So let's look at that . . .

If you like to play Scrabble, doing it to your utmost potential is great, but it's probably not worth the effort required. And likewise for taking all the time necessary to be the world's foremost ping pong player. Unless you're a professional, and do that for a living.

But there are some other areas, where you should never settle for second rate. Or accept less than you are capable of.

I think being a parent would certainly be one of those. That responsibility is so sacred, that you should continually learn, grow, and challenge yourself to get better. The only way you can be a good parent is to have this attitude.

The things that affect children have changed so much since we grew up, and things are changing so rapidly, that you must always be learning and adapting to provide your children with the guidance, love and support they need.

When I grew up, it was quite unusual for someone to bring a knife to school. Drugs were pretty prevalent, but it was mostly the less potent, less addictive kind. Most kids came from whole families, and the teachers knew each kid. Now look at today.

Guns are so prevalent in places like the U.S., that if a kid has an issue with someone, he or she can get access to a firearm in a matter of hours. Drugs have gone high tech, so they are easier to get, cheaper, very addictive, and very deadly. More than 50% of marriages today, end in divorce.

In many families still together, both the parents have two jobs. The number of kids raised in broken families is steadily increasing. And school budgets are straining, class sizes are getting larger, and the time a teacher has to get to know and help a student is getting shorter.

The programming a child faces today is simply mind-numbing. To win the most popular video games kids must kill between 20 and 50 people or things every ten minutes. If you don't stay abreast of what's popular, your child's reality could really be twisted.

The current crop of television shows available is simply beneath even contempt. The sensationalism, sexuality and vulgarity levels are so anti-prosperity and anti-humanity, that for an impressionable child to view them even for an hour a week is enough to warp and distort their minds for life. It's bad enough if an adult's idea of harmless entertainment is watching someone eat a cockroach, bludgeon someone senseless, or surprise their spouse with the news that they are sleeping with their sister. And mother.

If you start exposing someone to that programming when they are ten or eleven, trust me when I tell you, that you will not want them in the gene pool at 40.

A big part of being a good parent is staying abreast of the influences your children are being exposed to, and helping them cope with and manage those influences on their lives. This is easier said than done, I know.

The strong will of a child, the barrage of guilt a parent feels, and the fact that most parents are just too exhausted to oppose their children's desire to watch inappropriate shows or play violent video games can take over and cause the parent to cave in. But you can't. It's too important.   It comes down to courage and discipline. You have to create your own personal / family morals, and use your courageous efforts to enforce and stand by them. It is extremely difficult—but not impossible.

It means you have to do things that aren't fun or rewarding—like being your child's parent, instead of his or her best friend—but you do it, because you hope it will make a difference in the end.

And it's a never-ending process . . .

Kind of like being in love.

Which leads us to the next area to which you must devote super-human effort and dedication to growth if you want to make it work. And that is the investment necessary to have a committed relationship with someone you want to spend your life with. I can't even envision true prosperity, without having special people in your life, and especially that really special someone.

It starts out pretty easy. You adore them; they are infatuated with you. You even like those "quirky" things about them. You know, those little things they do when you meet them that you find cute—the same ones that make you want to strangle them after the relationship wears on.

Relationships take work. Lots of it. Loving relationships take even more work. Lots more of it. You have to grow, and you have to celebrate and nurture the growth of your partner. Even when this growth takes them into areas that you aren't interested in, or even may threaten you.

The reality is love is a verb—a series of actions you give and receive, which cause you to "be in love." Love only exists and evolves when you "do" love.

Love is your ultimate energy. An energy that you generously give when you first "fall in love." And when that fresh sensation goes silent, your discipline and effort must come forth. This is when the real work that supports a relationship begins.

I'm very blessed to have Drs. Ellyn Bader and Peter Pearson in my Mastermind Council. Ellyn and Peter run The Couples Institute in Menlo Park, California.

Their latest book, entitled "Tell Me No Lies," gives us some interesting insights into what it takes to move from accepting an "ok" relationship, versus developing a deep, meaningful and rewarding one.

This is when the relationship can and will withstand the test of time. But this won't happen if you don't make a major and continuous commitment to its being the highest good it can be. It is another case, like parenting, where the effort is worth the payback. It is a fight worth fighting.

And that's the point I want to make in all this . . .

That you must determine the areas of your life where you will not settle. I'm sure we can do a whole book on parenting, like we could on relationships. And many have.

But I bring them up here only in the context of using them as examples of the kinds of areas that are important ones to grow and develop to your maximum capacity to have a life of meaning.

So let's go back full circle to where we started . . .

We began this discussion with a look at work. Settling for a job, when you really should be an entrepreneur. Settling for good, when great is possible.

As you've probably discerned by now, I believe that your work is as important to you as your family and your relationships.

Now let's clarify that. I don't mean to say that you should miss the delivery of your first child because there was a staff meeting that day. Nor do I mean that the work you do at the office next Tuesday is as important as that father-daughter talk you need to have about drugs, dating and honesty.

But I think what you do is VERY important to who you are as a human being, and a big part of prosperity. And the roles you play as a parent or a partner are greatly influenced by the work you do, and how you do it.

Show me a guy who hates his job, and I'll show you a guy with a rocky marriage. Show me a mother who holds herself back for fear of upstaging her husband, and I will show you a mother who is being a horrible role model for her children.

People who tackle their work with joy, abandon and adventure will approach their marriage and family life the same way. I think everyone should work. Not because you need the money (although that's not a bad reason), but because your work allows you to develop, contribute and grow as a human being.

As you may know, I set up my life in a way that I thought I could retire at 40 years old. My goal was to live a life of leisure—racing cars, playing softball, and drinking out of a coconut. That lasted 'til I was 40 years and nine months old.

I realized very quickly how my intellect and other mental faculties could atrophy. If I would have done that for another six months, I would have been happy to sit at home evenings watching "Friends." Which would be a fate worse than death.

I think we need work that we are passionate about; work that has us ripping off the covers in the morning, ready to get to it. I have found that, and it contributes a tremendous amount to the fulfillment and joy I experience in life.

Make no mistake . . .

I have balance. I set boundaries so work doesn't consume me. I have softball leagues on Wednesday and Thursday nights, so I don't work those nights. Sometimes another night as well. I block off all nights for the Opera, as soon as the season schedule is released. I finish by early afternoon on Saturdays, and I don't work Sundays. (I have church in the morning, and another softball league in the afternoon.) If I do seminars on the weekend, I take off time in the middle of the week.

And the result is, I always look forward to Monday morning with great anticipation. I know I will have emails from my partner in Central Europe, and others from Oslo, London, Sydney, Singapore, Malaysia, or some other exciting place with details on a project. I'll have Daily Awakenings to write, and Online Seminars to brainstorm. I live my life with passion, and a great part of that passion comes from my work.

To reach a self-actualized state, I think everyone really does have to find work that does this for him or her. Which is not to say that every mother (or father) should work at a job.

I think of Debra Brandt-Sarif, another member of my Mastermind Council. Her full-time work is raising her three beautiful children, and it has as much passion and meaning for her, as my work does for me. Now when her kids are grown, she may go back to teaching, become a nuclear engineer, or develop a vaccine. But right now she has an obsession with her work of the moment. And that is the key to what we are talking about.

I believe . . .

You must have an obsession about something in order to succeed at it.

Now everybody has obsessions. The question is what obsesses you? And are your obsessions healthy ones or unhealthy ones?

If your obsession is darts, and you think all day about how you will prevail against the other guys at the pub that night, then that isn't going to take you very far towards a life of meaning. If your obsession is the Miami Blue butterfly, that may bring texture to your life, but you'd better have some more important areas you focus on as well.

The difference between people with empty lives and people with meaningful ones is simply the things they choose to obsess about.

Want to have a life of meaning? Want to leave mediocrity behind? Want to choose greatness and reach your highest good? Look at the things that you emphasize in your life.

Prosperity is not about things and "stuff." It is a mindset, and a way of living. It means being in touch with your spiritual side, and knowing the source of all the blessings that come to you.

You probably picked up this book because you are not yet manifesting all the prosperity you desire in life. That's good. I believe that we are never given a dream, without the resources to make it come true. Your situation may not be great at the moment, but it will not remain that way long, because you have a vision of where you want to be, and the person you want to become.

When you do the things we have discussed in this book, amazing things will begin to transpire in your life. It's impossible to travel *within,* and stand still *without.*

The masses don't understand how any of this works. They see only the apparent effect of things, and not the things themselves. They are the skeptics who will talk about "luck," and fortune and chance.

They don't see the sacrifice and work that go into manifesting true prosperity. They never notice the long journey—only the end result. In prosperity there are efforts, and there are results. The strength and commitment to the effort, are what determines the success of the result. It's not about chances, fate or luck. Prosperous people create their own chances, their own fate, and their own luck.

You may have a poor, low-paying job right now, or perhaps you don't even have a job. But once you have a dream, all that changes. You mentally build up your picture of a better life. This larger scope takes over your consciousness, and this changes your daily actions. You act differently. And people notice the difference.

Soon, your job can no longer hold you. It is cast aside as you move forward to bigger responsibilities. You are now a person of influence and action, because you have done what few can do. You have harnessed the power of the mind.

You will receive the vision of your heart—the exact results of your thoughts. You will be given exactly what you earn—no more, no less. You will become as small as your controlling desire, or as big as your boldest, most daring and imaginative aspirations.

I hope you aspire for a life of spiritual fulfillment, abundant health, enriching relationships, and outrageous wealth. It is all these things taken as one that constitute true prosperity.

The life you envision and program into your daily thoughts is the one you are going to live. So make it a prosperous one!

-RG

About Randy Gage

For more than 15 years, Randy Gage has been helping people transform self-limiting beliefs into self-fulfilling breakthroughs to achieve their dreams. Randy's story of rising from a jail cell as a teen, to a self-made millionaire, has inspired millions around the world.

This compelling journey of triumph over fear, self-doubt, and addiction, uniquely qualifies him as an undisputed expert in the arena of peak performance and extraordinary human achievement. His story and the way he shares it, demonstrate the true power of the mind over outside circumstances.

Randy Gage is a modern day explorer in the field of body-mind development and personal growth. He is the author of many best-selling albums including, *Dynamic Development* and *Prosperity* and is the director of www.BreakthroughU.com.

People from around the world interact and receive personal coaching from Randy through "Breakthrough U," his online coaching and success program. As Dean of BreakthroughU.com, Randy provides insight into how to overcome fear, doubt and self-sabotage to reach success and achieve the highest level of human potential.

For more resources and to subscribe to Randy's free ezine newsletters, visit www.RandyGage.com.

101 Keys to Your Prosperity

"Insights on health, happiness and abundance in your life."

You are meant to be healthy, happy and prosperous. Once you recognize and accept this, it is simply a case of learning the principles that abundance is based on.

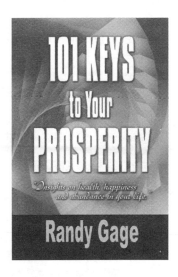

In this insightful book, Randy Gage reveals 101 keys to manifesting that prosperity in you own life. You will move from lack consciousness to living in the light of true abundance. You'll discover:

- What creates prosperity consciousness;
- The universal laws that govern prosperity;
- Why you should embrace critical thinking;
- The secret of creating a vacuum for good; and,
- What it takes to manifest prosperity on the physical plane.

Order the print book or downloadable eBook online at www.Prosperity-Insights.com

Quantity pricing for paperback book:

1–9 books	$7.00 each
10–99 books	$6.00 each
100–499 books	$5.00 each
500–999 books	$4.00 each
1,000 + books	$3.00 each

Order Online at **www.Prosperity-Insights.com** or call 1-800-432-4243 or (316) 942-1111

Accept Your Abundance!
Why You are Supposed to Be Wealthy

"Claim the Prosperity that is your Birthright."

Do you believe that it is somehow spiritual to be poor? One reading of this fascinating book will dissuade you of that belief fast. You'll understand that you are meant to be healthy, happy and wealthy.

Prosperity guru Randy Gage cuts through the religious dogmas to reveal why becoming rich is your spiritual destiny. You'll discover:

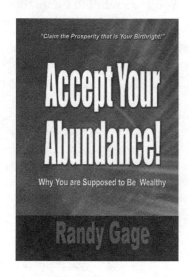

- Why poverty is a sin;
- What may be keeping you from your prosperity;
- Why being wealthy is your natural state;
- The difference between the way rich and poor people think; and,
- How to attract and accept your true abundance!

**Order the print book or downloadable eBook online at
www.Prosperity-Insights.com**

Quantity pricing for paperback book:

1–9 books	$7.00 each
10–99 books	$6.00 each
100–499 books	$5.00 each
500–999 books	$4.00 each
1,000 + books	$3.00 each

37 Secrets About Prosperity

"A revealing look at how you manifest wealth."

In this landmark book, prosperity guru Randy Gage unveils 37 little-known insights into the science of prosperity. Gage breaks it down into simple, understandable explanations, so you can apply the information in your life immediately to create your own prosperity. He reveals how he went from a dishwasher in a pancake house to a self-made multi-millionaire.

You'll learn:

- Why most people remain poor;
- How the rich leverage their prosperity;
- Why you should emulate certain business models;
- What separates broke, sick and unhappy people from the rich, healthy and happy ones; and,
- How you can manifest prosperity in all areas of your life.

Order the print book or downloadable eBook online at www.Prosperity-Insights.com

Quantity pricing for paperback book:

1–9 books	$7.00 each
10–99 books	$6.00 each
100–499 books	$5.00 each
500–999 books	$4.00 each
1,000 + books	$3.00 each

Prosperity Mind!

How to Harness the Power ofThought

"Brilliant Insights on health, happiness and abundance in your life."

Since "Think and Grow Rich," people have been fascinated with the power of the mind to accomplish great things. Now a recognized expert in human potential cracks the code on how you program yourself for prosperity!

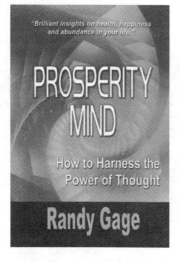

In this breakthrough book, prosperity guru Randy Gage reveals how you can actually program your subconscious mind to move from lack consciousness to prosperity thought. In it, you'll discover:

- How to identify self-limiting beliefs that hold you back;
- The 5 common expressions you probably use every day, which program you for failure on a subconscious level;
- How to practice the "vacuum law" of prosperity to attract good in your life;
- Imaging techniques to manifest things you want; and,
- How you can actually program your own subconscious mind for riches!

Order the print book or downloadable eBook online at www.Prosperity-Insights.com

Quantity pricing for paperback book:

1–9 books	$7.00 each
10–99 books	$6.00 each
100–499 books	$5.00 each
500–999 books	$4.00 each
1,000 + books	$3.00 each

Order Online at **www.Prosperity-Insights.com**
or call 1-800-432-4243 or (316) 942-1111

The 7 Spiritual Laws of Prosperity

"Live your life by the universal laws that govern health, happiness and abundance."

It is your birthright to be healthy, happy and prosperous. Accept this truth and it's simply a case of learning and living by the 7 Spiritual Laws that govern abundance.

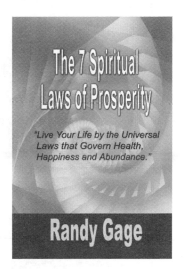

In this breakthrough and insightful book, Randy Gage reveals the secrets behind harnessing these laws to manifest your own prosperity. You'll learn about each of these Prosperity Laws and discover how to:

- Create a vacuum for good;
- Use imaging to get what you want;
- Find and keep your perfect soul mate;
- Use creativity to get the bills paid; and,
- Attract money, health and harmony to your life.

Order the print book or downloadable eBook online at www.Prosperity-Insights.com

Quantity pricing for paperback book:

1–9 books	$7.00 each
10–99 books	$6.00 each
100–499 books	$5.00 each
500–999 books	$4.00 each
1,000 + books	$3.00 each

The Prosperity Series
by Randy Gage

You are meant to be healthy, happy and prosperous. Once you recognize and accept this, it is simply a case of learning the principles that abundance is based on.

In this insightful series, you will move from lack consciousness to living in the light of true abundance.

Randy Gage reveals . . .

- What creates prosperity consciousness;
- The universal laws that govern prosperity;
- Why you should embrace critical thinking;
- The secret of creating a vacuum for good;
- What it takes to manifest prosperity on the physical plane; and,
- Why you are supposed to be wealthy.

Get all five books now and start living a life of abundance!

OrderThe Prosperity Series by Randy Gage online:
www.Prosperity-Insights.com

The Prosperity Series, 5 print books $30
The Prosperity Series, 5 eBooks $20
The Prosperity Series, all 5 print books and eBooks
Combination Special $47

Prosperity:
How to Apply Spiritual Laws to Create Health, Wealth and Abundance in Your Life
by Randy Gage

This album will help you uncover the subconscious "lack" programming you have that is holding you back. Then, you'll replace it with prosperity consciousness to manifest money, health, great relationships, happiness, and strong spiritual harmony.

True prosperity comes from understanding and living by the spiritual laws that govern our world. This album takes you through each of the Seven Spiritual Laws that govern prosperity—and shows you how to apply them. You will discover the ancient secrets to manifest prosperity in your own life.

You'll discover:

- Why you're supposed to be rich;
- The secrets of optimum health;
- How to get out of debt;
- The Seven Spiritual Laws you must live by;
- Your special powers for prosperity; and,
- How to image—then manifest—boundless, limitless prosperity.

This album will take you on a journey of spiritual enlightenment. You'll learn the practical applications so you can manifest prosperity in your life NOW! You'll learn about faith, the principle of attraction, and even how to use creativity to get the bills paid! This is the most specific, detailed and comprehensive album ever produced on how to become prosperous. **Don't you need it now?**

Prosperity: 8 CDs #A28CD $107
Prosperity: 8 audio-tape album #A28 $97

Dynamic Development
Achieve Your True Potential with the Dynamic Development Series
by Randy Gage

Do you live a life of joy—or simply get through the week? Can you communicate well with your family and co-workers, or do you struggle to be heard? Are you in open, honest and loving relationships, or do you hide behind a mask? How much more can you earn, learn, love and accomplish? *If you want to break out of self-imposed limitations and break through to your true potential—the **Dynamic Development Series** is the perfect resource for you.*

Instantly hailed when it was released as the ultimate self-development resource, this is a two-year program to nurture your personal growth and achieve your innate greatness. Each month you will receive an audiotape from human achievement expert Randy Gage with a lesson, and some "homework" to complete that month.

It's a continuing journey on your path of personal development. Each month will bring you on an in-depth study in some area of human achievement, whether body, mind or soul. You'll discover new truths about yourself and uncover old ones. You'll desire more, obtain more, and accomplish more . . . by becoming more.

Dynamic Development, Volume 1, 12 audio-tapes
#V2 $147

Dynamic Development, Volume2, 12 audio-tapes
V4 $147

BEST DEAL! Both Dynamic Development Volumes,
24 audio-tapes #V2V4S $247

Crafting Your Vision

Twelve success experts share their secrets to success . . .

As soon as this 12 audio-tape album was released, it was hailed as one of the greatest self-development tools since *Think and Grow Rich!* It gets to the real root cause of success or failure—the vision you create for yourself.

It's pleasing to your ego to assume your prosperity is not growing because of outside factors and other circumstances. **But the truth is—you are reaping the results of the vision you created!**

Your suffering, frustration or failure to reach goals is the result of a neutral or negative vision— just as the blessings in your life are the results of a positive vision. This is an immutable, unshakable universal law. Living the lifestyle of your dreams begins with crafting the vision of where you want to go. For without a clear, compelling vision you simply cannot achieve what you're truly capable of. And there simply is no  better resource to help you create an empowering vision for yourself than this amazing resource.

You'll learn how to craft your personal vision, how to design a vision big enough to encompass the visions of your people, and the steps to take on a daily basis to bring your vision to reality. You'll hear 12 complete programs on vision—recorded live—from 12 of the foremost experts on direct selling, recruiting and marketing.

This breakthrough album includes talks by:

Richard Brooke	Michael S. Clouse	Rita Davenport
John Milton Fogg	Matthew Freese	Randy Gage
Lisa Jimenez, M.Ed.	John Kalench	John David Mann
Jan Ruhe	Tom Schreiter	Tom Welch

When you finish, you'll really know how to craft and manifest the vision of where you want to go. Make sure this resource is in your personal development library. **Get it today!**

Crafting Your Vision–12 audio-tape album #A30 $97

Get Randy Gage As

The only ongoing education program specifically designed for your success! Get personal, individualized success coaching from **Randy Gage**. Join Randy as he helps you expand your vision, shatter self-doubt, and reach your true success potential. Breakthrough U is your opportunity to have Randy as your personal success coach— mentoring you through the mindset, consciousness, and daily actions necessary to reach the success you are capable of.

Initiate Level

This is level one of an amazing journey of self-discovery. Each day you will receive a "Daily Awakening" e-mail message filled with mind-expanding exercises and success lessons to teach you how to think like ultra-successful people think. In addition to these "mind aerobics," you'll receive marketing tips, prosperity secrets and just general success information on how to make it to the top.

You will also have access to the members-only forum on the site so that you can network with other success-minded individuals, and get an invitation to attend Randy's BreakthroughU Success Events.

This is priced inexpensively and is for the beginning success seeker. If you've faced adversity, are deeply in debt, maxed out on your credit cards, or simply starting the journey—this is the program for you. Randy created this level so that those who are down and out— but committed to getting "up and in" —have a vehicle to do so. It's a program to change your consciousness, one day at a time.

Now, if you are further along the path, and serious about reaching higher levels of success—you're ready to advance to...

Alchemist Level

Alchemy, if you'll remember, is the medieval philosophy of transmutation: converting base metals to gold. This is the level for you if you're seeking a transmutation in your life: converting base thoughts and desires into the thinking and actions that produce rich and prosperous outcomes.

(continued on the next page)

Your Personal Coach!

Like the Initiate Level, you will receive the Daily Awakening messages, access to the members-only forum, and an invitation to Randy's Success Convention. You will also receive:

- The "Alchemy Transmutation Kit" (with intro lesson, CDs and binder);
- Subscription to the monthly lessons;
- Access to the monthly online video seminars;
- Monthly Tele-seminars
- Two Personalized Consultations

Now, if you're serious as a heart attack about success, and want to get even more individualized and personal coaching...you might want to consider the pinnacle level:

Mastermind Council

This is Randy's "inner circle" of select consulting clients, business partners, and colleagues. They receive a package of benefits so lucrative, that it's never been offered anywhere before. Membership in the **Mastermind Council** gives you a chance to get the most personalized help and guidance from me individually— as well as interacting with some of the brightest entrepreneurial minds on the planet.

In addition to the same benefits as the Alchemist, you will also receive:

- Ten Personalized Consultations;
- The chance to participate in twelve live Mastermind Conference Calls a year;
- Members-only Council Updates; and,
- The chance to participate in the Mastermind Retreats each year.

For complete details go to:
www.BreakthroughU.com

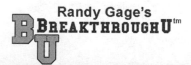

Randy Gage's Recommended Resources	Price	Qty	Total
Prosperity by Randy Gage Select: ☐ **audiotapes or** ☐ **CD's**	$97 (tapes) $107 (CDs)		
Dynamic Development Series Volume One by Randy Gage	$147		
Crafting Your Vision 12 audiotape album	$97		
Prosperity Series 5 books	$30		
101 Keys to Your Prosperity book	$7		
The 7 Spiritual Laws of Prosperity book	$7		
Prosperity Mind! book	$7		
Accept Your Abundance! book	$7		
37 Secrets About Prosperity book	$7		

United Parcel Shipping Table

Order Total	2-Day	Ground
$90.00 or under	$11.60	$5.50
$100.00-$200.00	$13.20	$6.00
$200.01-$300.00	$16.20	$6.50
$300.01-$400.00	$17.90	$7.00
$400.01-$500.00	$20.50	$7.50
$500.01- over	$23.00	$8.00

For Alaska, Hawaii, and Canada, figure the total of your order, plus the regular shipping cost, and add 10%. For foreign and overseas orders, figure the total of your order, plus the regular shipping cost, and add 20%

Subtotal

$_____

Shipping (see chart)

$_____

Terms: 60-day money back guarantee! Contact us within 60 days of your invoice date if, for any reason, you're not 100% satisfied with any product you've received from us. Product must be in re-sellable condition. Customer Service: 1-800-946-7804 or (316) 942-1111

$_____
TOTAL

PAYMENT TYPE: ☐ **Visa** ☐ **MC** ☐ **AMEX** ☐ **Discover** or ☐ **Cash** ☐ **Check**

Please print clearly

Credit Card # _ _ _ _ _ _ _ _ _ _ _ _ _ _ _ _

Expires: (MM/YY) ____/____ Signature:_____

Full Name:

Address: Apt./Suite#

City: **State:** **Zip:** **Country:**

Phone: **Email:**

Customer Service: Prime Concepts Group
1807 S. Eisenhower St. • Wichita, Kansas 67209-2810 USA
1-800-432-4243 or (316) 942-1111
Fax: (316) 942-5313